Meditative Solos for Clarinet

CREATIVE SOLOS FOR THE CHURCH MUSICIAN

Created and Compiled by Ed Hogan

Moderate Difficulty

enhanced D

Audio Accompaniment Tracks, Piano Parts, and Rhythm Parts included on the Enhanced CD

PUBLISHING COMPANY

Contents

All Creatures of Our God and King

Music: *Geistliche Kirchengesange, 1623*
Arranged by Marty Parks
Solo Arranged by Ed Hogan

Smoothly

Marcato

The Love of God

Music by FREDERICK M. LEHMAN
Arranged by Kyle Hill
Solo Arranged by Ed Hogan

Trust Medley
'Tis So Sweet to Trust in Jesus*
Trust and Obey**
Standing on the Promises***
Leaning on the Everlasting Arms****
Only Trust Him*****

Arranged by Camp Kirkland
Solo Arranged by Ed Hogan

With Energy

♩ = ca. 126

*Music by WILLIAM J. KIRKPATRICK.
**Music by DANIEL B. TOWNER.
***Music by R. KELSO CARTER.
****Music by ANTHONY J. SHOWALTER.
*****Music by JOHN H. STOCKTON.

"Trust and Obey"

"Standing on the Promises"

"Leaning on the Everlasting Arms"

"Only Trust Him"

Higher Ground

Music by CHARLES H. GABRIEL
Arranged by Michael Lawrence
Solo Arranged by Ed Hogan

It Is Well with My Soul

Music by PHILIP P. BLISS
Arranged by Kyle Hill
Solo Arranged by Ed Hogan

Cross Medley
Glory to His Name*
At Calvary**

Arranged by Michael Lawrence
Solo Arranged by Ed Hogan

"Glory to His Name"

"At Calvary"

O the Deep, Deep Love of Jesus

Music by THOMAS J. WILLIAMS
Arranged by Marty Parks
Solo Arranged by Ed Hogan

Resurrection Medley

Joyful, Joyful, We Adore Thee*
Crown Him with Many Crowns**

Arranged by Marty Parks
Solo Arranged by Ed Hogan

"Crown Him with Many Crowns"

"Joyful, Joyful, We Adore Thee"

All That Thrills My Soul

Music by THORO HARRIS
Arranged by Michael Lawrence
Solo Arranged by Ed Hogan

Christmas Medley

Angels We Have Heard on High*
What Child Is This?**
Come, Thou Long-expected Jesus***

Arranged by Richard Kingsmore
Solo Arranged by Ed Hogan

Acoustic Feel ♩ = ca. 98　　"Angels We Have Heard on High"

*Music: Traditional French Carol.
**Music: Traditional English Melody.
***Music by ROWLAND H. PRICHARD.

"What Child Is This?"